CORE LIBRARY OF US STATES

South Carolina

BY JAMIE KALLIO

CONTENT CONSULTANT
Edward Lee, PhD
Professor of History
Winthrop University

Core Library

An Imprint of Abdo Publishing
abdobooks.com

abdobooks.com

Published by Abdo Publishing, a division of ABDO, PO Box 398166, Minneapolis, Minnesota 55439.

Printed in the United States of America, North Mankato, Minnesota.
052022
092022

Cover Photo: Shutterstock Images
Interior Photos: Sean Pavone/Shutterstock Images, 4–5, 45; Red Line Editorial, 7 (South Carolina), 7 (USA); Shutterstock Images, 10, 19 (flag), 19 (flower), 22–23, 27; FLHC25/Alamy, 12–13, 43; George A. Kenna/Shutterstock Images, 17; Bonnie Taylor Barry/Shutterstock Images, 19 (bird); iStockphoto, 19 (dog); Elizabeth Foley/Shutterstock Images, 19 (tree); Kim McGrew/Shutterstock Images, 28; Page Light Studios/Shutterstock Images, 30–31; Stacie Stauff Smith Photos/Shutterstock Images, 34; Emma McIntyre/Getty Images Entertainment/Getty Images, 36–37

Editor: Katharine Hale
Series Designer: Joshua Olson

Library of Congress Control Number: 2021951574

Publisher's Cataloging-in-Publication Data

Names: Kallio, Jamie, author.
Title: South Carolina / by Jamie Kallio
Description: Minneapolis, Minnesota : Abdo Publishing, 2023 | Series: Core library of US states | Includes online resources and index.
Identifiers: ISBN 9781532197826 (lib. bdg.) | ISBN 9781098270582 (ebook)
Subjects: LCSH: U.S. states--Juvenile literature. | Southeastern States--Juvenile literature. | South Carolina--History--Juvenile literature. | Physical geography--United States--Juvenile literature.
Classification: DDC 975.7--dc23

Population demographics broken down by race and ethnicity come from the 2019 census estimate. Population totals come from the 2020 census.

CONTENTS

CHAPTER ONE
The Palmetto State 4

CHAPTER TWO
History of South Carolina 12

CHAPTER THREE
Geography and Climate 22

CHAPTER FOUR
Resources and Economy 30

CHAPTER FIVE
People and Places 36

Important Dates. 42

Stop and Think. 44

Glossary. 46

Online Resources. 47

Learn More 47

Index 48

About the Author. 48

CHAPTER ONE

THE PALMETTO STATE

The SkyWheel slowly turns, towering 200 feet (61 m) above the Atlantic Ocean. The SkyWheel is a huge Ferris wheel. People relax in its gondolas and look out the glass windows. They point in delight as different colors from the SkyWheel flash against the night sky. Many riders have spent the day down below at Myrtle Beach. They built sandcastles, swam in the ocean, and sunbathed in the hot sun. This is summertime in South Carolina, the Palmetto State.

The SkyWheel is one of many attractions in Myrtle Beach.

ABOUT SOUTH CAROLINA

South Carolina is in the southeastern region of the United States. The state is bordered by North Carolina to the north and northeast and Georgia to the west. The Savannah River runs between Georgia and South Carolina. To the east of the state lies the Atlantic Ocean. South Carolina has 187 miles (301 km) of Atlantic coastline. There are also the Sea Islands. These are barrier islands that extend south along the Atlantic Coast down to Georgia.

South Carolina is home to a variety of landscapes. The Blue Ridge Mountains run along the northwest corner of the state. They got their name because they appear blue in color. People visit the mountains to enjoy cool temperatures, hiking trails, and scenic waterfalls. Spartanburg and Greenville are in northwestern South Carolina.

Central South Carolina is made up of rolling hills. The cities of Aiken and Columbia are there. Columbia is

MAP OF SOUTH CAROLINA

South Carolina has many important cities and famous landmarks. What does this map show you about the locations of South Carolina's major cities? How does this map help you understand South Carolina's geography?

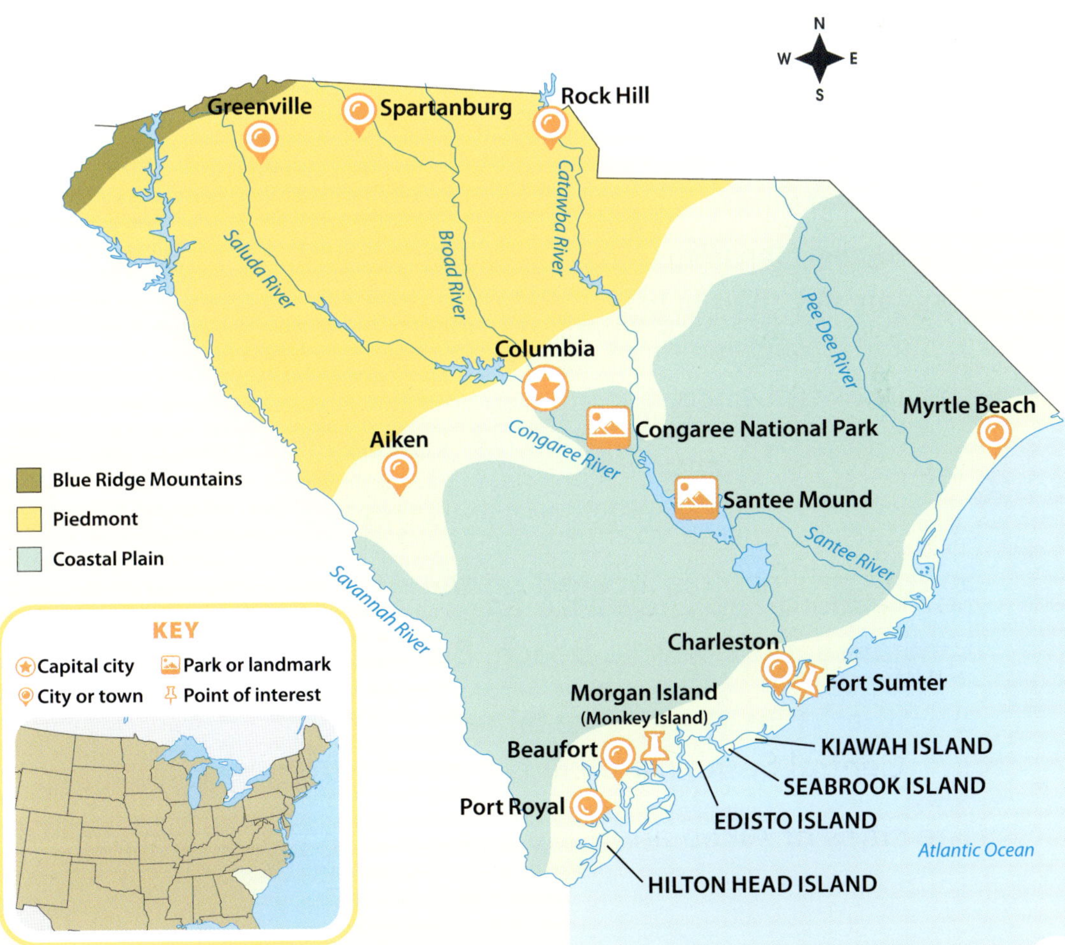

MONKEY ISLAND

There is an island off the coast of Beaufort where no humans live. The island is officially named Morgan Island, but it is often called Monkey Island. This is because almost 4,000 rhesus monkeys roam free there. In 1979 the monkeys were moved to the island from a primate research facility in La Parguera, Puerto Rico. The South Carolina Department of Natural Resources owns the island. Humans are not allowed to visit, but they can sometimes see the monkeys by boat.

the capital and second-largest city in the state. Horse racing, famous restaurants, and kayaking on the Saluda River draw visitors to this area.

Eastern South Carolina is made of the Coastal Plain and Coastal Zone. The southern part of this region is known as the Lowcountry. Charleston is the largest city in South Carolina. It is located on the Atlantic Coast and is a major seaport. Myrtle Beach, Beaufort, and Port Royal are other cities in the Coastal region.

South Carolina has many rivers. Three large river systems are the Santee, the Savannah, and the Pee Dee. Smaller rivers such as the Saluda, Catawba, Broad, and Congaree are part of these systems. All drain into the Atlantic Ocean.

EXPLORING THE PALMETTO STATE

South Carolina is known for its beaches. The Grand Strand is 60 miles (97 km) of beaches between Georgetown and Little River. The Grand Strand gets 19 million visitors a year. The Sea Islands provide even more beaches.

PERSPECTIVES

BARBECUE

Many people claim that barbecue was invented in South Carolina. Supporters of this theory say when Spanish explorers brought pigs to the New World, American Indians demonstrated how to cook them. The American Indians were already cooking animals in large open pits. The Spanish supplied the pigs, American Indians supplied the pits, and barbecue was born. Barbecue pitmaster Jack Waiboer says, "[American] Indians were cooking that way when the hog came to America, and that's how pit-cooked barbecue came about."

Hilton Head is the most popular of the Sea Islands. There are more beach resorts located on other Sea Islands. These include Kiawah Island, Seabrook Island, and Edisto Island.

South Carolina is called the Palmetto State because of its state tree. The palmetto grows along the Atlantic Coast from North Carolina to the Florida panhandle. The palmetto is on South Carolina's state flag.

The state has a long and rich history. Before Europeans set foot on the land, approximately 29 different American Indian peoples inhabited the area. Charleston is one of the oldest cities in the country. It was founded in 1670. With South Carolina's history, beaches, ancient cypress trees, and so much more, this state has lots to explore.

Charleston is known for historic buildings.

CHAPTER TWO

HISTORY OF SOUTH CAROLINA

Humans have lived in South Carolina for approximately 11,000 years. Ancient peoples known as Paleo-Indians lived along the riverways during the last ice age. They were nomadic. They hunted ice age animals such as mammoths and mastodons. As the climate warmed, these large animals started to die off. The nomadic peoples adapted to the warming climate. They began to stay in one place.

The Catawba people have lived in South Carolina for thousands of years. This Catawba family was photographed in South Carolina in 1908.

SANTEE MOUND

Visitors to the Santee National Wildlife Refuge will discover a 30-foot (9-m) hill. This hill is known as the Santee Indian Mound. The Santee people lived along the Santee River for thousands of years. The mound was used as a burial and ceremonial site. Years later, the mound was also the site of the British Fort Watson. The mound is estimated to be 1,000 years old.

Paleo-Indians were the ancestors of later American Indian peoples in South Carolina. These later peoples include the Cherokee, Catawba, and Yamassee. The Catawba call themselves *yeh is-WAH h'reh*, which means "people of the river."

COLONIAL TIMES

Spanish explorers were the first Europeans to come to South Carolina. In 1566 they established the colony of Santa Elena on Parris Island. After years of conflict with American Indians, the Spanish relocated to Saint Augustine, Florida.

In 1663 King Charles II of England sent eight noblemen to settle the Carolinas. In 1670 the English founded Charles Town on the bank of the Ashley River. After ten years, the colonists moved across the river and set up what is now Charleston. In 1712 the colony was split into North Carolina and South Carolina.

The colonists built large plantations on the land to grow rice, tobacco, and indigo. The plantation owners exported these crops for large profits. In order to work such large pieces of land, the British settlers enslaved people from Africa and other places to do the labor. By the 1700s, Black enslaved people made up most of South Carolina's population. The white plantation owners grew very wealthy. South Carolina became one of the richest colonies in the United States.

Tensions had been growing between Britain and the 13 American colonies. The colonists did not want to pay taxes imposed by the British government. They decided to separate from Britain. This resulted in the Revolutionary War (1775–1783). More than 200 battles took place in South Carolina. The colonists won, creating the United States of America. In 1788 South Carolina became the eighth state.

SLAVERY AND THE CIVIL WAR

Some of South Carolina's plantations grew cotton. Picking cotton was slow, hard work. In 1793 Eli Whitney invented the cotton gin. This device made it easier to pick cotton. Soon cotton became America's top-selling crop. The demand for enslaved workers increased. Plantation owners wanted to grow more cotton. They wanted to use the lands of American Indians. In 1830 Congress passed the Indian Removal Act. The act forced American Indians to leave their homes and live on reservations in the West. In 1838 the government forced American Indians to march 1,200 miles (1,900 km) to their new homes. The route came to be known as the Trail of Tears. Thousands of American Indians died on this long, hard trip.

After taking control of Fort Sumter from the Union, Confederate soldiers used the fort to keep the Union Navy away from Charleston. Today the fort is a national historic site.

The Southern states' economies depended on the labor of enslaved people. But views about slavery were changing throughout the country. Northern states wanted to abolish slavery. The plantation owners of the South did not. This led South Carolina to secede from the United States, or Union, in 1860. Other Southern states did the same. These states became the Confederacy. On April 12, 1861, the Confederates fired the first shot at Union troops at Fort Sumter, near Charleston. The American Civil War began. It lasted until 1865, when the Union defeated the Confederacy. An estimated 620,000 Americans died in the war. Roughly 18,000 soldiers from South Carolina were killed.

RECONSTRUCTION AND JIM CROW

Between 1865 and 1877, people worked to rebuild the country after the Civil War. This period is called Reconstruction. Union troops were sent to occupy the South and to aid in rebuilding. The Confederate states were allowed to rejoin the Union. To do this, each state had to write a new constitution. The states also had to ratify the Thirteenth and Fourteenth Amendments to the US Constitution. These amendments abolished slavery and granted citizenship to formerly enslaved people.

PERSPECTIVES

TWO MOTTOS

South Carolina has two state mottos. The first is "*Animis opibusque parati.*" It means "Prepared in mind and resources." This Latin phrase first appeared on South Carolinian money in 1776. In 1777 the state used the motto and the palmetto tree on the front of its state seal. The second motto is *"Dum spiro spero."* This is also a Latin phrase, meaning "While I breathe, I hope." It appears on the back of the seal. Both mottos express South Carolina's confidence and optimism for the future.

SOUTH CAROLINA
QUICK FACTS

Each US state has its own unique history and culture. How do South Carolina's state nickname and mottos represent its history? Did you find any of South Carolina's state symbols surprising?

Abbreviation: SC
Nickname: The Palmetto State
Mottos: *Animis opibusque parati* (Prepared in mind and resources) and *Dum spiro spero* (While I breathe, I hope)
Date of statehood: May 23, 1788
Capital: Columbia
Population: 5,118,425
Area: 32,020 square miles (82,931 square km)

STATE SYMBOLS

State bird
Carolina wren

State flower
Yellow jessamine

State dog
Boykin spaniel

State tree
Palmetto

South Carolina rejoined the United States in 1868. But racism in the South continued. White supremacist groups formed during this time. These groups terrorized Black people and those who supported them. Politicians in Southern states, including South Carolina, passed racist Jim Crow laws. These local laws separated Black and white people in public spaces. In South Carolina, Black people were not allowed on many beaches. They had to drink from separate water fountains and attend separate schools. Politicians also restricted Black people's voting rights. The civil rights movement started in the 1950s. It was a mass protest against discrimination in the Southern states. The movement brought about the Civil Rights Act of 1964 and the Voting Rights Act of 1965. These acts prohibited discrimination and guaranteed people's right to vote regardless of their race or ethnicity.

GOVERNMENT

South Carolina's state government has three branches. The executive branch carries out laws. The governor is the head of the executive branch and is elected by the people. The legislative branch makes laws. The judicial branch interprets laws and makes sure the laws follow the Constitution.

American Indians continue to live in South Carolina today. The Catawba Indian Nation is the only federally recognized tribe in the state. The Catawba tribal lands are in York County.

EXPLORE ONLINE

Chapter Two discusses South Carolina's American Indian history. The article at the website below goes into more detail about the Catawba people. Does the article answer any questions you had about these people and their history?

THE CATAWBA NATION: ABOUT THE NATION

abdocorelibrary.com/south-carolina

CHAPTER THREE

GEOGRAPHY AND CLIMATE

The landform regions across South Carolina are diverse. Sassafras Mountain in the northwestern Blue Ridge region is the highest point in the state, reaching 3,553 feet (1,083 m) above sea level. The Piedmont region is home to gently rolling hills. The Sandhills stretch diagonally from southwest to northeast in the center of the state. They are made of clay and sand. The Coastal Plain is the largest landform in South Carolina. It covers two-thirds of

Lake Jocassee is in Devils Fork State Park. The park is in the Blue Ridge Mountains.

the state. The Coastal Plain is divided into the Inner and Outer Coastal Plains. This area is good for agriculture. The Coastal Zone is only 10 miles (16 km) wide. It stretches along South Carolina's coast.

WEATHER AND CLIMATE

The climate of South Carolina is subtropical. This means winters are mild, and summers are hot and humid. Sometimes winters can be cold. The coldest temperature ever recorded was −19 degrees Fahrenheit (−28°C) in January 1985. Snow falls mostly in the mountains and the Piedmont. The highest temperature recorded in South Carolina was 113 degrees Fahrenheit (45°C) on June 29, 2012. Precipitation happens mostly in spring and summer, with approximately 49 inches (124 cm) of rain falling in the state per year.

Tornadoes are frequent in the Southeast. Carolina Alley is known for high tornado activity. The area includes north Georgia, South Carolina, and

North Carolina. South Carolina averages 11 tornadoes each year.

Hurricanes also affect South Carolina. These are severe rotating storms. They form over tropical or subtropical waters in the warm, moist air. Their wind speeds reach 74 miles per hour (119 km/h) and higher. In South Carolina, coastal cities such as Charleston and Myrtle Beach are at the highest risk for hurricane damage.

PERSPECTIVES

HURRICANE HUGO

Hurricane Hugo hit South Carolina on September 22, 1989. The day before it made landfall, the weather was sunny and clear. Government officials feared a huge loss of life if people did not evacuate their homes. Charleston County council member Linda Lombard made an appearance on the news. She stated that the approaching hurricane was the size of South Carolina. "If you want to leave Charleston, please leave now," she said. "Please leave now." Hugo's winds were between 135 and 140 miles per hour (217–225 km/h). The storm killed 35 people and caused approximately $8 billion to $10 billion in damage.

ANGEL OAK

The Angel Oak is located right outside of Charleston on Johns Island. It is one of the oldest living trees in the Southeast. The tree is estimated to be anywhere from 300 to 500 years old. It stands 65 feet (20 m) tall. Its branches provide 17,000 square feet (1,580 sq m) of shade. The tree's name comes from the Angel Estate, which was owned by Justus and Martha Waight Angel. Local stories also claim that the ghosts of past enslaved people appear as angels around the tree.

When hurricanes strike, the state is also at risk from storm surges, high winds, and flooding. Hurricane season in South Carolina runs from June to November.

PLANTS AND ANIMALS

South Carolina is the sixth-most forested state in the United States. It has approximately 13.1 million acres (5.3 million ha) of forests covering 68 percent of the state's land. One of the most common trees is the palmetto. Bald cypress and sweet gum trees also grow in abundance. Dogwood and magnolia trees

A Venus flytrap's leaves can close, trapping insects inside. The plant digests insects for nutrients that aren't available in the soil.

grow colorful blooms. The yellow jessamine is the state flower. Its vines cover fences and trees with bright-yellow flowers. The yellow jessamine attracts hummingbirds and butterflies. Carnivorous plants such as the pitcher plant and the Venus flytrap grow in the coastal wetlands.

South Carolina has many kinds of mammals. These include small animals such as squirrels and skunks.

Birds such as the great blue heron call South Carolina home.

South Carolina is also home to large predators such as wolves, mountain lions, and black bears. Marine animals live along the Atlantic Coast. These include dolphins, sharks, and whales. In the brackish marshes and swamps, reptiles are plentiful. American alligators live here. South Carolina is also home to venomous snakes, including copperheads, cottonmouths, and several kinds of rattlesnakes.

There have been more than 438 bird species recorded in South Carolina. The most common birds include the northern cardinal, the Carolina wren, and the Carolina chickadee. Seagulls are the most dominant birds along the coast.

STRAIGHT TO THE SOURCE

In 1683 colonist Louis Thibou wrote a letter to his family and friends in France about the geography and climate of South Carolina:

> *I shall give you details about this country and its mode of life, and first of all I shall describe to you that it is a wooded country with lovely savannas or plains crossed by fine rivers very full of fish in which anyone who likes can fish and with enough oysters to feed a kingdom. . . . In short I assure you it is a fine climate, very temperate and very healthy, where one feels very fit. Everything you can imagine growing in France or in England grows here. Carolina has good earth, nothing barren about it and it only needs to be cultivated.*

Source: "Letter from Louis Thibou to Friends and Family in France, 1683." *Teaching American History in South Carolina*, n.d., digital.scetv.org. Accessed 16 Sept. 2021.

BACK IT UP

The author of this passage is using evidence to make a point. What is that point? Write a paragraph describing the author's main idea. Then add two or three pieces of evidence that support the author's point.

Thank You
YA'LL
COME
BACK

CHAPTER FOUR

RESOURCES AND ECONOMY

Agriculture is still the top industry of South Carolina, but it has changed over time. Today much of the state's income is produced from livestock. These animals include turkeys, cattle, and hogs. Valuable crops are tobacco, soybeans, cotton, and corn. Honey and pecans are produced in the state. And even though Georgia is famous for peaches, South Carolina produces more of them. The state produced 67,330 tons of peaches in 2020. Fishing is

Strawberry Hill Farms in Cooley, South Carolina, grows strawberries, peaches, and other produce. Peaches are a major crop in South Carolina.

also an important industry. Shrimp is the most popular seafood in the United States. It is also South Carolina's top catch. The state brings in clams, crabs, and oysters too.

PERSPECTIVES

TRAWLING FOR SHRIMP

South Carolina's largest fishery is the shrimp industry. The Lowcountry has two kinds of shrimp. Brown shrimp are harvested from May through August. White shrimp are harvested from September to December. Shrimp are caught using large boats called trawlers. Trawling for shrimp is hard work. If the weather is bad and the fishers catch nothing, they don't get paid. But that doesn't stop local fisherman Captain Lee Hickey. "I love it out here," he said. "The troubles of life melt away and it's just you and the boat, the water and the shrimp."

Natural resources such as granite, limestone, and gold are mined in South Carolina. Forestry is one of the top industries in the state. Hardwoods are used for lumber, and softwoods are used to make paper.

MANUFACTURING

South Carolina's economy suffered

after the Civil War. Manufacturing began to build it back up. The textile industry was a major industry from 1880 into the 1930s.

Now South Carolina is known for its advanced manufacturing. Aerospace and automotive manufacturing are major industries. This includes vehicle parts and automotive machinery. The state also produces pharmaceuticals.

BIRTHPLACE OF SWEET TEA

Summerville, South Carolina, is believed to be the birthplace of sweet tea. Sweet tea is a cold drink that consists of water, tea, and lots of sugar. Sweet tea is sweetened when the tea is hot. This allows all of the sugar to dissolve. The tea is then chilled and served over ice. Summerville is a historic town located near Charleston. People can visit shops and businesses along the town's Sweet Tea Trail for tea-themed goodies. One stop on the trail is Mason, a 15-foot-tall (4.5 m) mason jar that can hold up to 2,524 gallons (9,554 L) of sweet tea.

TOURISM

Millions of people visit the Grand Strand, Charleston, Greenville, and Columbia. They are drawn to South Carolina's warm weather, beaches, and hundreds of golf courses. Tourism generates approximately $15 billion annually. More than 10 percent of the population works for the tourism industry. In 2019 visitors to Myrtle Beach generated $145 million. South Carolina has become a thriving and important state.

FURTHER EVIDENCE

Chapter Four talks about agriculture in South Carolina. What was one of the main points about agriculture? What evidence is included to support this point? Watch the video at the website below. Does the video support the information in the chapter? Does it present new evidence?

THE JOURNEY OF FOOD–FROM FARM TO TABLE

abdocorelibrary.com/south-carolina

Myrtle Beach is a major beach vacation destination.

Off-White

CHAPTER FIVE

PEOPLE AND PLACES

The Palmetto State has a population of more than 5 million people. White people who are not Hispanic or Latino make up approximately 64 percent of the population. Black people make up 27 percent of the population and Asian people approximately 2 percent. American Indian people make up 0.5 percent and Hispanic or Latino people 6 percent of the population.

Chadwick Boseman was a famous South Carolinian. He is well-known for playing the superhero T'Challa in *Black Panther*.

PERSPECTIVES

THE GULLAH

The Gullah are a group of Black Americans from South Carolina and Georgia. They are the descendants of enslaved people taken from West Africa to the South's Sea Islands. They live in small communities along the Atlantic Coast. They speak Gullah, which is a blend of English and West African languages. They have passed down African folktales, handicrafts such as sweetgrass baskets, and traditional rice and seafood meals for generations. "This culture is part of your culture. You cannot have the complete story of American history without South Carolina history," says Gullah native and educator Anita Singleton-Prather. "You cannot have South Carolina history without Gullah history."

THINGS TO SEE AND DO

Nature lovers who visit Columbia can white water raft on the Saluda River or hike at Congaree National Park. The city also has a vibrant arts scene with museums, theaters, and more. Restaurants offer everything from fine dining to southern comfort food such as barbecue.

In 2019 nearly 7.3 million people visited Charleston. The city is full of history and culture, along with miles of beaches and water activities. There are more than 1,400 historic buildings in Charleston. The Charleston Museum was founded in 1773, making it America's first museum.

SPORTS AND CELEBRITIES

People in South Carolina enjoy a variety of sports. Myrtle Beach and Hilton Head are known for their golf courses. South Carolina has no major league sports teams. But it has ties to the Carolina Panthers. The Panthers are a National Football League team. They play in Charlotte, North Carolina. In 2019 the team announced it would build a training facility and headquarters across the border in Rock Hill, South Carolina. College sports are also very popular. There is heated competition between the University of South Carolina Gamecocks and the Clemson University Tigers.

Many famous people come from South Carolina. Musician James Brown is called the "Godfather of Soul." Brown was inducted into the Rock and Roll

Hall of Fame in 1986. Chadwick Boseman starred as Brown in the 2014 movie *Get On Up*. Both men were born in South Carolina. In 2018 Boseman starred in *Black Panther*, a superhero movie that became a worldwide hit. He passed away in 2020 at age 43.

South Carolina has a long history, beautiful landscapes, and a wide variety of cultural and recreational activities. Residents and visitors alike enjoy all of these features of the state. South Carolina offers something for everyone.

ALTHEA GIBSON

Althea Gibson was born in Silver, South Carolina, in 1927. As a child, she preferred sports over studies. She was very good at table tennis. She moved on to playing tennis and received a sports scholarship to attend Florida A&M University. In 1950 Gibson was the first Black tennis player to compete at the US National Championships. She also competed at Wimbledon in 1951. Gibson's success was a significant gain for other Black athletes in the country.

STRAIGHT TO THE SOURCE

Chadwick Boseman grew up in Anderson, South Carolina. After his death, people in the town wanted to honor his legacy. Downtown Anderson has many public artworks on display. The city created a public art fund to honor Boseman with new art. Mayor Terence Roberts spoke about the fund at an exhibit where local artists honored Boseman. He said:

> *We want to continue to push that momentum; when you come to downtown, you see our art. . . . Chadwick Boseman was the ultimate artist. He was world-known and we think it's important to push in this direction for a couple different reasons, to honor his legacy but to continue the momentum that we have in our community.*

Source: Sophia Radebaugh. "Anderson Uses Artwork to Honor Chadwick Boseman." *WSPA 7 News*, 22 Oct. 2020, wspa.com. Accessed 17 Sept. 2021.

WHAT'S THE BIG IDEA?

Take a close look at this passage. What connection is Mayor Roberts making between Boseman and art? What does the passage tell you about Boseman's importance to his community?

IMPORTANT DATES

11,000 years ago

Paleo-Indians first inhabit South Carolina.

1566

Spanish explorers establish Santa Elena on Parris Island.

1670

The English found Charles Town. Ten years later, the colony is moved to present-day Charleston.

1775–1781

The 13 colonies fight the British for freedom in the Revolutionary War.

1838

The US government forces American Indian peoples from the southeastern United States to move to western lands on a journey known as the Trail of Tears.

1860
Tensions over slavery lead South Carolina to secede from the Union. Other Southern states follow and form the Confederacy.

1865
The Confederacy is defeated and the American Civil War ends.

1950
Althea Gibson becomes the first Black tennis player to compete at the US National Championships.

2019
Myrtle Beach generates $145 million in tourism.

STOP AND THINK

Why Do I Care?

Chapter Four discusses the fishing industry in South Carolina. Maybe you don't like seafood or have never tried it. What do you think would happen if South Carolina stopped catching shrimp? How might it affect the state's economy? How would it affect the United States?

Another View

Chapter Five discusses the Gullah people and their culture. As you know, every source is different. Ask an adult to help you find another source on the Gullah. Write a short essay comparing and contrasting the new source's point of view with that of this book's author. What is the point of view of each author? How are they similar and why? How are they different and why?

Surprise Me

Chapter Two discusses South Carolina's history. After reading this book, what two or three facts about South Carolina did you find most surprising? Write a few sentences about each fact. Why did you find each fact surprising?

You Are There

This book discusses the popularity of South Carolina's beaches. Imagine you are riding the SkyWheel at Myrtle Beach. As you look out the windows, what do you see? Write a letter to your friend describing the experience. How would you describe the sights in a letter to friends back home?

GLOSSARY

abolish
to officially end something

barrier island
a small, narrow island that protects the mainland from storms

brackish
salty; used to describe water

export
to ship and sell products to another region or country

pharmaceutical
a medicine or drug

plantation
a large farm where the workers live on-site

ratify
to sign or give formal consent to an agreement or document

secede
to leave a political union

storm surge
the rise of the sea due to storms

textile
cloth produced by weaving or knitting

white supremacist
a person who falsely believes white people are better than people of other races

ONLINE RESOURCES

To learn more about South Carolina, visit our free resource websites below.

Visit **abdocorelibrary.com** or scan this QR code for free Common Core resources for teachers and students, including vetted activities, multimedia, and booklinks, for deeper subject comprehension.

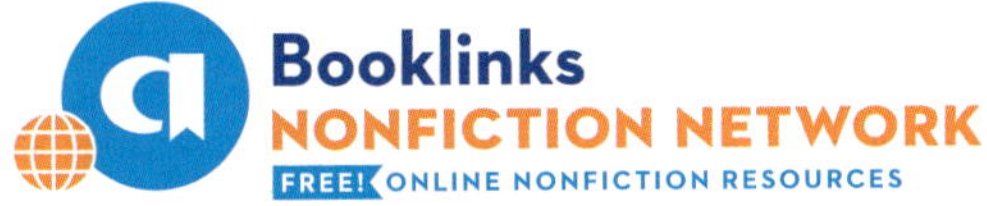

Visit **abdobooklinks.com** or scan this QR code for free additional online weblinks for further learning. These links are routinely monitored and updated to provide the most current information available.

LEARN MORE

Krull, Kathleen. *A Kid's Guide to the American Revolution.* HarperCollins, 2018.

Seidel, Jeff. *South Carolina Gamecocks.* Abdo, 2019.

INDEX

agriculture, 15–16, 24, 29, 31, 35
American Indians, 9, 13–14, 16, 21, 37
animals, 8, 9, 13, 19, 27–28, 29, 31–32

Blue Ridge Mountains, 6, 7, 23
Boseman, Chadwick, 40, 41
Brown, James, 39–40

Carolina Panthers, 39
Charleston, 7, 8, 11, 15, 17, 25, 26, 33, 35, 38–39
civil rights movement, 20
Civil War, 17–18
Coastal Plain, 8, 23–24
Columbia, 6–8, 19, 35, 38

Gibson, Althea, 40
Grand Strand, 9, 35
Greenville, 6, 7, 35
Gullah, 38

hurricanes, 25–26

Jim Crow laws, 20

Monkey Island, 7, 8
Myrtle Beach, 5, 7, 8, 25, 35, 39

palmetto tree, 5, 11, 18, 19, 26

Reconstruction, 18
Revolutionary War, 15–16

Sassafras Mountain, 23
Sea Islands, 6, 7, 9–11, 38
slavery, 15–18, 26, 38
Spanish explorers, 9, 14
Spartanburg, 6, 7
Summerville, 33

Thibou, Louis, 29
tornadoes, 24–25

About the Author

Jamie Kallio is the author of many nonfiction books for children. She is also a librarian in the south suburbs of Chicago, Illinois. She doesn't like shrimp, but she loves barbecue!